SICILY
art and history

Published and printed by

plurigraf

NARNI - TERNI

Index

Photographs: Archivio Plurigraf - Barone - Bianchi -
             Italia Paolo - Scala - Senzanonna -
             Sperandei - Vescovo
Aerial photos authorization: S.M.A. n. 506 del 20-9-91

Introduction

This illustrated guide has been put together with the intention of offering a wide view of the most interesting and important part of Sicily: a souvenir, an image of its innumerable and extraordinary beauties, though it certainly has not been possible to include all of them, and to assign to each one the space it deserves. We have tried, however, to distill the essence of this region and to trace its most characteristic features, and we hope to have achieved this by marking an itinerary through the nine provincial capitals, and through other centres of artistic, social, economic and tourist interest in general.

Sicily, the largest of the Italian islands, has a triangular shape (from which it perhaps derives its ancient name of Trinacria); the land is mostly mountainous and is characterized by volcanic phenomena, most active around the centre of Mount Etna (the largest volcano in Europe), and in the Aeolian Islands, all of which are of great interest. Sicily was populated even in prehistoric times, as attested by the many necropoli and grottoes scattered around the whole territory. Later it became the object of Greek colonization, thanks to which its cities achieved power and prosperity, and it inherited the most important traits of that civilization, known indeed as an important part of Magna Graecia - Greater Greece. To this period belong the splendid archaeological remains scattered almost everywhere on the island: at Siracusa, Gela, Agrigento, Selinunte, Segesta, Imera, Solunto.

Then came the people from outside: the Byzantine rule, and the brief Arab rule. Longer and more important was that of the Normans (11th-12th centuries), who gave to this region great moments in its art and culture, as we can see through numerous and valuable examples. A most meaningful example is to be found in the various palaces, in particular the one called dei Normanni (of the Normans) in Palermo and churches: that of Cefalù and that of San Giovanni degli Eremiti (St. John of the Hermits), and the truly extraordinary one of Monreale. These Norman structures with their particular architectural style and their refined mosaic decoration, still today adorn many cities.

The Normans were followed by the Swabians. In particular, it was under the rule of Frederick II that Palermo became an important cultural centre: it will suffice to remember the famous Sicilian School, which had such a great part in initiating Italian literature in the vernacular. The art of this period is also well represented, especially in the numerous castles existing here, there and everywhere (to be remembered is the Ursino Castle in Catania, built for Frederick II himself), whereas other buildings remain linked to previous tendencies, except when outside influences came to bear.

The brief Anjou rule (1266-1282), a period of bad government characterized by oppression, inquisitorial proceedings and enfeoffment of lands, was broken off by the revolt of the Sicilian Vespers (1282).

Then began the Aragon Reign. In the meantime, Sicily had gradually lost its important role in the Mediterranean, and declined even more after the Aragonese reduced it definitively into the orbit of Spanish politics. There were some strong reactions and revolts, such as those of Palermo and Messina round the middle of the 17th century, but these were severely repressed. Art, too, suffered from this rule for a long time, but in the 15th century, because of the commercial exchanges with the rest of Italy, and the presence of such a strong personality as that of Antonello da Messina, there was a golden period in Sicilian painting.

Still in the field of art, and in particular that of architecture, the 17th and the 18th centuries are largely and richly represented: the churches, the palaces, the villas, are built according to the styles typical of that time; whole cities, such as Noto, reflect these characteristics.

The 19th century saw in this region the succession of the Savoia family, the Austrians and, principally, the Bourbons: at this point the history of Sicily becomes linked to, and a part of, that of the rest of the peninsula, thanks to Garibaldi, who, at the head of his Mille (or Thousand men), clashed with the Bourbon troops, driving them out once and for all.

The region then became a part of the Kingdom of Italy.

Its life, however, was anything but easy, since the centralizing forces of the new State and the laws which ignored historical reality, both economic and social, created hardships and problems of such gravity that they have yet, in large measure, to be solved.

Sicily's economy is still largely agricultural: the main cultivations are wheat, grapevines, olive trees, vegetables and fruit. In recent times, however, the industrial sector has seen a great development, in particular the mining industry: sulphur, potassium salts, asphalt and oil are extracted. This activity is linked to a considerably gifted chemical industry. Unfortunately, many problems connected with the phenomenon of emigration still remain unresolved, with the existence of harshly depressed areas, and the lack or insufficiency of adequate work machinery. A large segment of the population devotes itself to fishing: there is an abundance of swordfish, tuna, eels, sardines, in the waters surrounding the island.

There are numerous and very interesting folkloric activities and, more simply, all those aspects most characteristic of the local colour thanks to which Sicily has acquired its strongly individual personality.

Sicily has been, since 1946, a region with a special constitution.

So now, guided by the perfume of orange blossoms, and accompanied by the sound of the jew's-harp, let us begin to learn something of this magnificent region.

Palermo

The situation of this town is enchanting, at the foot of Mt. Pellegrino, in the plain of the "Conca d'Oro" (Golden Valley), before the wide and wonderful harbour.

Palermo is beautiful thanks not only to its situation and very mild climate, which helps the growth of luxuriant vegetation, but also to its many monuments, works of art and gardens, which make it a first-class tourist centre.

It was a Carthaginian colony, but in 254 passed under the domination of the Romans, who called it Panormus (literally "all harbour") referring to the wide coastal arch on which it lay. So it became the first town and harbour of the island. Under the Saracens and Normans it flourished so much that it became under Frederick II of Swabia the most active cultural centre in Italy. It was here that the vernacular poetry originated. Palermo, however, declined under the Angevins, the Aragonese, the Spaniards and Bourbons (1415-1860). After it was annexed to the Kingdom of Italy (1860), the town flourished again and became rich, though during the last war the area of the harbour, many churches and houses were almost completely destroyed. Some of these buildings could not be restored.

The various historical periods of the town, especially the Norman and Baroque periods, have left traces in the town-planning and monuments.

Palermo is a trully exceptional town. The more one knows it, the more one discovers priceless beauties and treasures. It is the capital town of the island.

THE CHURCH OF ST. JOHN OF THE HERMITS

The Church of St. John of the Hermits is a great example of the Norman art, peculiar and picturesque as it is, thanks to its particular forms and vivid colours. The church, whose construction began in 1132 by order of Roger II, looks like a squat and squared building surmounted by small red domes. The interior, with only one nave, is quite bare. From it one can get to the remains of a squared building, which was probably a mosque. Very suggestive is the small cloister with arches resting on columns arranged in pairs, built in later age.

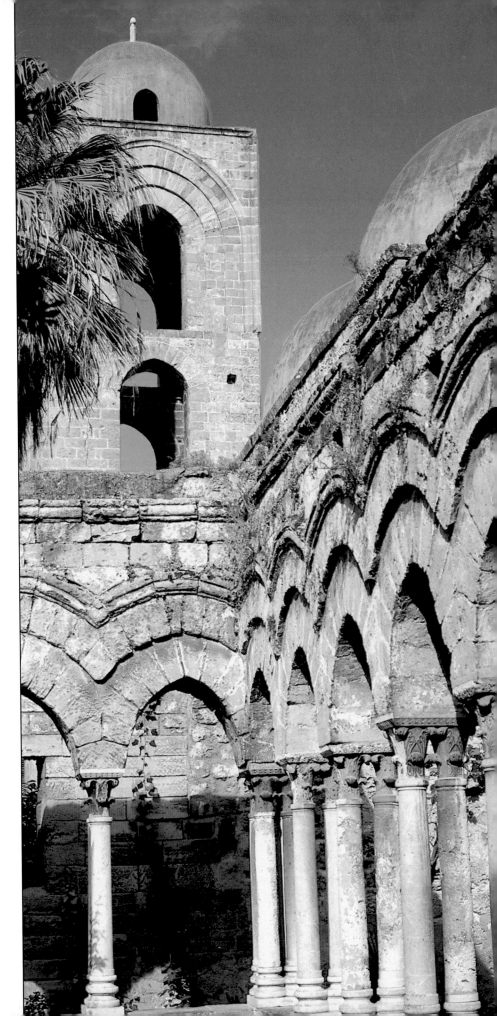

St. John of the Hermits: Details of the Cloister.

THE CATHEDRAL

The large and imposing structure of the Cathedral of Palermo, in which the various building periods have led to a mixture of different styles.

Begun in 1185, it was subjected to additions and alterations in the 14th, 15th and 16th centuries. The interior was remodelled from 1781 to 1804, and the dome was designed by Ferdinando Fuga (1699-1781). The facade, dating to the 14th-15th century, is connected by two large pointed arches to the original bell-tower, medieval in its lower and 19th century in its upper part.

The 15th century portico is formed of three pointed arches springing from columns with a tympanum above decorated with Gothic motifs. The portal, surmounted by a 13th century mosaic Madonna, is the work of Antonello Gambara (1426).

The Latin cross-shaped interior has a nave and two aisles. The first and second chapels in the right aisle house the imperial and royal tombs, including the Tomb of Frederick II and that of his consort Constance of Aragon. In the sixth chapel are preserved the urns with the mortal remains of the Saints of Palermo. The Sanctuary contains carved choir-stalls, a masterpiece of Gothic-Catalan art (15th century). From the apse we can enter the Sacristy of the Canons, and thence the New Sacristy in which the Cathedral's Treasury is displayed in a number of glass-cases; it consists of liturgical vestments of the 16th-18th centuries, objects of goldsmith's work, enamelwork and embroidery.

The Cathedral: Details of the façade.
Facing page: *The interior of the Cathedral.*

PIAZZA VIGLIENA (THE FOUR CANTI)

Formed in 1609 at the wish of the viceroy, the Marquis of Vigliena, by rounding off the corners of the two main streets of the old town where they crossed one another: Via Maqueda and Corso Vittoro Emanuele (the old "Cassero"). The two arteries running at right-angles determine the division of the old town into four large, populous quarters. The octagonal square presents, on its four sides or "cantoni", a splendidly rich and ornate example of Baroque architecture. The first tier, at street level, is decorated with four fountains surmounted by statues symbolizing the seasons, works by the sculptors Nunzio La Mattina and Gregorio Tedeschi.

(The architectural plan was begun to designs by Giulio Lasso and finished under the direction of Giuseppe De Avanzato in 1620).

The niches of the second tier contain statues of the Spanish kings Philip II, III and IV and of the Emperor Charles V, precious works by the sculptor Giovanni Battista d'Aprile. In the niches of the upper tier, the statues of the four saints and protectors of Palermo - S.S. Cristina, Oliva, Agata and Ninfa - tower above the square. The coping is decorated with imperial and royal coats of arms.

On the west side of the four "cantoni" stands the Church of San Giuseppe dei Teatini, one of the richest and most valuable works of 17th-century Sicily, built over and incorporating the other Church consecrated to our Lady of Providence (La Madonna della Provvidenza). Erected in 1612 to plans by the architect Giacomo Besio, it was he who designed the simple facade upon which stands the statue of St. Gaetano, founder of the Theatine order. The dome (1724) is the work of Giuseppe Mariani, and the bell-tower is by the architect Paolo Amato.

Church of St. Joseph of the Teatines - Interior.
Left page: *The Cathedral apse.*

THE GREAT PRETORIA FOUNTAIN

Situated in the homonymous square, it was made by Francesco Camilliani in 1554-1555 for a Florentine villa, but it was sold in 1573 to the town of Palermo, which put it here. It lies on steps and is surrounded by banisters. It is round, with two concentric planes separated by a ring of water. In the centre there is a marble pillar surmounted by a "putto" with a cornucopia (horn of plenty). Around it there are statues of pagan deities, allegories, herms and heads of animals pouring water into the big annular basin and into smaller basins.

MASSIMO THEATRE

It is one of the largest theatres in Europe.
It was planned by G.B. Basile in 1875. It is in neo-classi-cal style, with a flight of steps leading to a Corinthi-an hexastyle pronaos; on the sides of the steps there are two bronze lions.

THE CHURCH OF MARTORANA OR HOLY MARY OF THE ADMIRAL

It was built by order of George of Antioch, admiral of Roger II, in 1143. It was given in 1433 by King Alfonso to a monastery founded by Elvisa Martorano, after whom it was named. Through the centuries it was badly damaged by destructions and adaptations, but now it has been restored to its original structure. This church is a true jewel of Norman art.

Above, and on the following page: *The Church of the Martorana.*
Below: *Massimo Theatre.*

The Church of the Martorana: Detail of "the Benediction of Christ".

Facing page: *The Church of the Holy Spirit.*

THE PALAZZINA CINESE (THE CHINESE VILLA)

The so-called Chinese Villa, designed by G. Venanzio Marvuglia, was erected inside the Park of the Favorita by King Ferdinand III of the House of Bourbon. The King and his consort Maria Carolina lived there for a long period while Naples was occupied by the Napoleonic troops.
More recently it was the home of Lord Nelson and Lady Hamilton. In the square in front of the building stands the gate of the Villa, which also serves as the main entrance to the Park of the Favorita, a vast estate of magnificent gardens, acquired by Ferdinand III of the House of Bourbon in 1799.

THE BOTANICAL GARDEN

Founded in 1789 under the patronage of King Ferdinand IV who financed the undertaking. The central building, known as the "Ginnasio" is the work of the French architect Leone de Fuorny, while the frescoes that adorn the dome are by Giuseppe Velasquez. The statues

and the stucco work are by Gaspare Ferriolo, Domenico Dané and Vitale Tuccio. In the side buildings, the "Calidario" and the "Tepidario" (by Venanzio Marvuglia), there are fine collections of herbaria, both Sicilian and from every part of the world. The importance (at European level) and the splendour of this institution are revealed by a visit to the garden (approx. 25 acres) with its profusion of extraordinary exotic and European plants.

THE CHURCH OF THE SANTO SPIRITO OR THE VESPRO

Easter Monday, 31st March 1282. As was their custom, the citizens of Palermo were gathering in the fields around the Church of the Holy Spirit to celebrate the feast. An undisciplined group of French soldiers was searching the men as they thronged to the festival, since no Sicilian was allowed to bear arms. Imprudently, the soldiers decided to search the women, too, tearing off their clothes in the process. Seldom has lack of

prudence given rise to more terrible consequences. The men, outraged and insulted by the behaviour of the soldiers, did not wait to take their revenge. They slew the French soldiers to a man, and the sparks of revolt spread at once through the whole of Sicily. Very few French survived the ensuing massacre and those who managed to save their lives were driven off the island.
The revolt of the Vespers sparked off a long war which spread into Calabria and onto the sea, brought to a close in 1302 with the peace of Caltabellotta. The Church is today incorporated into the site of the cemetery of S. Orsola, founded by Archbishop Gualtiero Offamilio in 1178 during the reign of William II and restored by Giuseppe Patricolo in 1882. Conceived on square lines, pointed arches decorated with multi-coloured lava and tuff inlay run along its side. The outside of the apse is decorated with intertwined ribbing and the outlines of windows. The solemn interior, suggestive in its austerity, is on a Latin plan, consisting of a nave and two aisles divided by columns and pillars, a wider sanctuary and three apses.

THE CHURCH OF SANTA MARIA DEL GESÙ

At the foot of Monte Grifone, from which Giuseppe Garibaldi, hero of Sicilian liberty, descended at the head of his men, lies the little cemetery where the patricians of Palermo are laid to rest. A steep flight of steps running up the side of the terrace gardens with their monuments to the dead (including the tomb of Luigi Mercantini, author of the hymn sung by Garibaldi and his followers) leads to the little square that lies in front of the Church of Santa Maria del Gesù.

Erected in 1429 by Beato Matteo da Agrigento, it was attached to an ancient Franciscan friary.

The facade has a splendid marble portal with figures of the Saints holding the "Credo" panels.

To the left, the 15th century Gothic-Catalan portal of the Grua-Talamanca Chapel inside which, on two spans with ribbed vaulting, are the remains of 15th century frescoes depicting the life of a saint. The cloister with the remains of the 15th century monastery belonging to the original building.

From the "Belvedere" which lies above the buildings on the mountainside, the visitor can enjoy one of the finest views of Palermo with Monte Pellegrino and Monreale.

CHURCH OF THE MAGIONE

This Church, founded in 1150 by Matteo d'Aiello, was originally granted to the Cistercians, passing in 1193 to the Order of the Teutonic Hospitallers. Beside the Church the remains of the 12th century cloister may be seen. The interior consists of a nave and two aisles divided by marble columns supporting pointed arches.

THE NORMAN PALACE

Now the building is the seat of the governing body of the Sicilian region. In ancient times, Phoenician-Punic and Roman works of defence were placed in the area. In the 11th century the Arabs reinforced the structures and built "the Palazzo degli Emiri".

The Normans enlarged it notably, calling in Byzantine and Arab artists in order to adorn its appearance. Thanks to the Normans and then to the Swabians this magnificent and sumptuous royal palace became the most important centre of civilization and culture in Europe. The Emperor Frederick II, a clever and enlightened sovereign, turned his court into a centre for poets, writers, philosophers and scientists. From these rooms "the first lyrics of the Italian language took wing'". The palace is composed of various sections built at different times. The great facade was built during the 16th and 18th centuries by the viceroy Vigliena. On the lefthand side the Pisan tower and St. Ninfa tower rise up. It is the seat of the Astronomical observatory, which represents the Norman part of the building, as does the splendid Cappella Palatina, which brings together the oldest mosaics of 1143 in the most original Byzantine style and King's Hall with its walls and vaults covered by extraordinary mosaics of 1170 which depict figures of animals and trees adorned with the finest

decorations. The Cappella Palatina was built in the centre of the building by order of Roger II in 1132, was completed in 1140 and dedicated to St. Peter. Through the centuries the building was subjected to many rebuildings and modifications which leads us to believe that only a little of the original Arab-Norman building remains.

In 1921, further works of renewal and restoration of the oldest parts began, ordered by the Ministry of Education. Many rooms were restored such as: the Stanza dei Tesori, with its characteristic jars fitted into the floor which contained gold coins and other riches belonging to the Norman and Arabian rulers; the political prisons were made of thick, solid walls with narrow slits; the Sala degli Armigeri is an austere military-like room with a beautiful cross-vault. The royal flats are on the upper floor of the building and are now the Headquarters of the Sicilian Parliament. The Parliament room or Hercules room with Giuseppe Velasquez's frescoes, the dining-room and the viceroy's room stand out particularly.

The Norman Palace: Details of the courtyard.

+PASTOR PETRE
+ALES BOS HOMO VULTU SLEO PRECONES SIMUL ISTI +
VIRGO MARIA FELIX QUE VERBIS CREDIS NEC CORDE SUPERBIS
SPONGIA LIGNEA CRUX CLAVI CORONA DANT EX PARTE METUM COGUNT ET FUNDERE FLETUM PECCATOR PLORA CUM VIDERIS HEC ET
PARTE STAT INDE DEXTRA MICHAEL GABRIEL QUE SINISTRA UT MAIESTATI SINT DE SERVIRE PARATI +

Photograph opposite: *The Palatine Chapel - Apse.*
Palatine Chapel: Detail of the Christo Pantocratore (Christ Omnipotent).

The Norman Palace: Hall of Ruggero II.
This page, above: *King Ruggero delivers the founding documents of the Palatine Chapel to the Cantor Simone.*
Below: *The Genio of Palermo holds a medallion which has the portraits of King Ferdinand of Bourbon and Maria Carolina.*

THE CHURCH OF
ST. JOHN OF THE LEPERS

The Church of St. John of the Lepers is one of the ancient monuments from the Norman period.

Founded by Roger I in 1070, it was completed only a century later in 1150 when a neighbouring leper hospital was attached to it.

THE FRIARY AND
CATACOMBS OF THE
CAPUCHINS

Essentially a cemetery lying beneath the friary; a most macabre spectacle is created by the eight thousand or so mummified corpses to be found there. The friary dates back to 1621, and the practice of mummifying the citizens of Palermo of a certain social rank before burial in the so-called "Capuchinian Catacombs" dates from this time.

The friary houses an international college for overseas missionaries. The library contains fine collections of rare Arab editions and of Greek and Latin oratorios of the Migne.

The civic cemetery, situated near the friary, is the final resting place of G. Tomasi di Lampedusa, author of the novel "Il Gattopardo".

THE REGIONAL GALLERY
OF SICILY

The Abatellis Palace has been since 1954 the seat of the Regional Gallery of Sicily, where are kept paintings, sculptures and archaeological material once kept in the Regional Museum. The building, in late Gothic style, planned by Matteo Carnevalieri, is square-shaped. It has a courtyard surrounded by a portico with two rows of arches and a facade with two side towers, on whose walls mullioned windows open out.

The National Gallery offers many testimonies of Sicilian artistic production during the 15th, 16th and 17th centuries, and of the many changes due to its contacts with Italy, Provence and the Low Countries.

The two-storeyed Gallery occupies 16 halls, apart from the Atrium and the Portico, where some sculptures are kept.

Among the most important works kept here we may mention: the «Annunciation», the «Nativity», the «Presentation in the Temple», the

«Flight into Egypt» of the school of Antonello Gagini; a sarcophagus of Cecilia Aprile dating back to 1495, attributed to Laurana; the «Triumph of Death», probably a work of Pisanello's collaborators; a Spanish-Arab jar, with a white background and golden decorations, dating back to the 13th-14th century, fished out of the sea of Palermo; the Bust of Eleonora of Aragon, made by Laurana; many works by Tommaso De Vigilia, a painter of Palermo; the «Annunciation» by Antonello of Messina; a «Madonna and Child», by Leonardo of Pistoia.

Apart from the Regional Gallery, there is in Palermo also the Regional Archaeological Museum.

THE REGIONAL ARCHAEOLOGICAL MUSEUM

The Regional Archaeological Museum is situated in Olivella Square. Together with that of Syracuse, it constitutes the most important collection of works concerning ancient Sicily.

In the three-storeyed Museum there are very interesting and valuable archaeological remains, some of which, originating from necropolises in the area of Chiusi, constitute the Etruscan collection.

In the many halls are kept objects found in the sea-depths of Western Sicily (amphorae, stone, lead and iron anchors); sculptures and epigraphs dating back to the Greek and Roman ages; bronze, terracotta and ceramic works from the excavations of Solunto, Termini Imerese, Tindari. The Ettore Gabrici Hall and the Selinunte Hall keep almost all the material from Selinunte. Among all these works the most important ones are some very fine sculptures, which are thought to be the most ancient ones of Selinunte, such as the triad Artemis-Latona-Apollo and Europa abducted by Jupiter, who had taken the shape of a bull; three metopes of the C temple, discovered in 1823 and today restored in such a way that some traces of painting can be seen; two half-metopes of the F temple and four metopes of the E temple. Four halls are occupied by the Etruscan collection with stone sarcophagi, alabaster urns, cinerary statues, memorial stones and vases made of bucchero, a special kind of Etruscan black-coloured terracotta.

The Capuchin Catacombs.

Above, left: *Bust of Eleanor of Aragon (Laurana)*
Rigth: *The Malvagnà triptych - a detail.*
Below: *The Sicilian Regional Gallery - entrance.*
Facing page: *Antonello da Messina's "Annunziata".*

SANCTUARY OF SAINT ROSALIA

A wonderful route, notable for the incomparable landscape through which it passes, leads to Monte Pellegrino, a magnificent rocky promontory jutting out into the Gulf of Palermo, which it delimits on the western side. It commands splendid panoramic views. It was in this wonderful natural setting that the Sanctuary of Saint Rosalia was built in 1625. It stands close to the cave where the Saint, who lived in the 12th century, used to pray.

The site of the Sanctuary, which has long been associated with the fervent devotion of the people of Palermo, is the constant goal of pilgrimages to pay homage to the patron Saint of the city. The cult dates back to the 17th century when a terrible plague epidemic was warded off thanks to the intercession of Saint Rosalia who, according to tradition, appeared at this spot during this period and indicated the place where her bones, by which the miracle would be performed, were buried.

The Sanctuary and the Convent were erected adjacent to a natural cavern where the Saint led a solitary life completely dedicated to prayer and meditation.

A statue portraying Saint Rosalia has

been installed in the cave; offered as a gift by king Charles III of Bourbon, it shows her recumbent covered by a gilded mantle (sculpted by G. Tedeschi in the 18th century). The water that flows down the walls of the cave is considered miraculous.

The church stands at the foot of a flight of stairs. An entrance-hall richly embellished with stone plaques and inscriptions forms the vestibule to the cave itself.

Monreale

The beautiful town rises on the slopes of Mt. Caputo, only 8 kilometres from Palermo.

It is very interesting to visit it, since its Cathedral and the nearby Cloister are the highest and most magnificent examples of Norman art.

The Cathedral, whose construction was begun in 1174 by order of William II, has kept its splendour till now.

The façade has an 18th century portico with three arches surmounted by banisters, and situated between two quadrangular towers. The ogival portal has bronze doors made by Bonanno Pisano (1186), with biblical scenes in relief. The magnificent and suggestive interior has its walls almost entirely covered with wonderful mosaics, ceilings with finely painted uncovered beams, and a floor made of porphyry and granite. This is the largest and most outstanding mosaic in Italy and the biggest one in the world after St. Sophia in Constantinople. It covers an area of 6,430 sq. mets. and is more than two thousand metres larger than the one in the Basilica of San Marco in Venice, inserted as it is in the monumental body of a place of worship defined as a "jewel" or work of art which is unique in the whole world and set amongst the most enchanting of natural beauties.

Every corner of the walls of the Cathedral is covered with figures and decorations on a glimmering

base of gold which make up 130 pictures which tell the story of the divine will for universal salvation.

The set of pictures starts with a representation of the Creation and continues with the stories of the patriarchs Noah, Abraham, Isaac and Jacob. The central aisle bears 42 panels on which the artists of the age painted episodes of the Old Testament, beginning with the creation as told in Genesis. They represent scenes from the Old and New Testaments. In the central apse is the image of the Pantocrator (Almighty), practically a copy from that of Cefalù. The main altar made of silver and bronze, one of Valadiers' works, the treasure including many relics, and in St. Benedict's chapel "St. Benedict in glory", made by Ignazio Marabitti in 1776, are all very valuable works. From the terraces of the Cathedral, which can be reached by a door situated at the beginning of the right aisle, one can see all the "Conca d'Oro" (Golden Valley). On the right side of the Cathedral there is the Cloister dating back to the 12th century. It is square, with each side 47 metres long. It has a portico delimited by ogival arches supported by 228 columns arranged in pairs and variously adorned with mosaics and carvings. This beautiful Cloister is really enchanting.

The half length figure of the Blessing Christ dominates above, in the dome of the middle apse. Below there is the Madonna and Child on a throne, with Angels, Apostles and Saints. The cycle of the splendid and solemn mosaic decoration, made by local and Venetian artists, starts from the middle nave, above on the right, with the Stories from Genesis, which continue on the inside wall of the facade and on the left side of the nave. Then follow the Stories of Christ, which run from the arches of the Sanctuary to the right aisle, to the left one and the two walls. In the left apse there is the figure of St. Paul with the Stories of the Saint on the adjacent wall. In the apse on the left and on its wall is St. Peter with Stories. Then in the Sanctuary, on the left, «William II receives the crown from Christ»; on the right, «William II offers the cathedral to the Virgin».

Monreale
Facing page: *The apse of the Duomo (cathedral).*
This page, above: *Christ on a throne, crowns William II.*
Below: *History of Genesis - Overall view.*
Next page: *The Benediction of Christ.*

THE SMALL CLOISTER

Also striking are the Small Cloister (the so-called "Chiostrino"), which are incorporated in the southern corner of the Cathedral's large Cloister. This is a square enclosure formed by three pairs of columns on each side, supporting pointed arches with double moulding. The columns rest in part on a plain stone basement - like the rest of the cloister -, and in part on a square podium with projecting marble string-courses of great chiaroscural effect.

At the centre of these small cloister is a graceful fountain. Rising from the centre of the circular basin is a chevron-decorated column, from the top of which water wells. The columns of the surrounding colonnade are almost all decorated with polychrome mosaics forming variegated geometric motifs. The capitals, too, like those elsewhere in the Cloister, are of great beauty; they are carved with bas-reliefs representing a variety of subjects.

As a whole this tiny jewel of medieval art, and the silence in which it is enveloped, arouses deep emotions: a sense of meditation and serenity prevails. But the visitor is struck too by the extreme elegance of the decorations, the minuteness of their detailing, the extreme delicacy of their colours.

Solunto

Founded by the Phoenicians during the first Punic penetration in Sicily, Soloeis rose on an upland plain at the top of Monte Catalfano. Allied to Carthage during the First Punic War, it voluntarily surrendered to the Romans. It was rather an unimportant town until the Romans rebuilt it. The city ruins are of remarkable archaeological importance (following its destruction by the Saracens). These ruins are dominated by Greek and Roman remains. The monumental remains are represented by the Ginnasio with an Atrium, peristyle and some Doric fluted columns with the trabeated style still partly preserved, the big house of Leda with the portrayal of the swan myth inside it, and some houses with mosaic floors and painted walls. On the tops of the hills are the ruins of the theatre, where part of the stage and some parts of the stalls have been preserved intact. Many of the archaeological remains are conserved in the Museum of Palermo and in the local Antiquarium.

Because of its position, it's possible to have a wonderful view. The eye ranges from the blue outline of the mountainous massif of the Madonie, to the coast dotted with the white houses of the coastal villages of Solunto, Porticello, S. Flavia, S. Elia to Cefalù and the Aeolian Islands.

Imera

The ancient Himera, the most western of the Greek towns on the northern coast of Sicily, was founded in the 7th century B.C. by the inhabitants of Zancle (Messina). It was destroyed in 409 B.C. by the Carthaginian Hannibal. Recent excavations have brought to light two small archaic sanctuaries and an important Doric temple, of which only the large steps and the bases of the columns remain. The temple was probably erected to commemorate the victory of Jelon of Syracuse and Theron of Agrigento over the Carthaginians near the river Himera in 480 B.C. It was 55,91 metres long and 22,45 metres wide. It was a peripteral hexastyle and had a pronaos. It is very similar to the Athenalon of Syracuse, built in the same period.

Cefalù

The situation of this town is suggestive thanks to the wonderful and picturesque contrast between sea and rock. It lies on a promontory and a slightly undulating area, at the foot of a massive rock steeply sloping down to the sea.

The ancient name of Cefalù, Cephaloedium, probably comes from the shape of this rock, which looks like a head. The town was ruled by the Greeks, Romans, Byzantines and Normans. The latter made it an independent diocese embellishing it very much. Of this past, the Fortifications near the coast, the regular town-planning with an evident medieval mark, and the Norman Cathedral still remain.

The Cathedral, one of the most beautiful churches in Sicily, was built by order of Roger II. The construction was begun in 1131 and went on for the entire century. In the outside the church presents a high transept and three apses with small arches and blind loggias on the upper part. In the background is the rock. The street before the Cathedral, Mandralisca Street, leads to the Mandralisca Museum, so called because it keeps the material collected by Baron Enrico Piraino of Mandralisca in the last century. The Museum includes an archaeological section with prehistoric tools and Greek vases; a scientific section with a collection of more than 20,000 shells; a very rich numismatic collection, which includes, apart from the coins from the Mint of Cefalù, those of the main towns of ancient Sicily; a Picture-gallery, housing the «Portrait of an unknown person» by Antonello of Messina, and works by other skilful artists, such as Dionislo Calvaert, Francesco Mieris, Domenico Fetti and Antonello De Saliba.

This page:
*Cefalù: The coast at Torre Caldura.
Cefalù: a typical view.*

Following page: *Views of the Cathedral of Cefalù.*

The beautiful cloister of the Cathedral can be reached from the left aisle. It is surrounded on three sides by a portico with columns arranged in pairs, and capitals supporting ogival arches. This cloister, too, reflects the vicissitudes of the construction of the Cathedral. The most important part of the capitals, however, seems to be contemporary to it and is rich in very beautiful motifs.

The mosaic representing Christ Pantocrator, huge and terrible, with his book of mandatory laws, is in the dome of the apse.

The figure of Christ was made in 1148, together with the other mosaics covering the apse, the walls of the presbytery and the ribbed vault of the Cathedral. It strikes the visitor not only for its huge size, but also for its sad look, almost immersed in painful meditations, and for its solemn pose. The wrinkles on the face, the curls of the beard and the lapels of the mantle make the figure less dramatic, though it keeps that tone of suffering humanity.

From this figure comes that, very similar, of the Pantocrator represented in the dome of the apse of the Cathedral of Monreale.

The town is a frequented bathing resort, thanks to its mild climate and its beautiful and peculiar landscape.

On the crag dominating Cefalù one can visit the Rock with the Prehistoric Sanctuary, also called temple of Diana, a megalithic construction dating back to the second century B.C. In the environs, the ruins of Imera, the Sanctuary of Gibilmanna and Termini Imerese are places worth visiting.

Inside the Cathedral: The apse and a detail of the Christo Pantocratore (Christ Omnipotent) mosaic.

Segesta

Magnificence and solitude reign in this place. Among the mountains rise the imposing Temple and Theatre, the only witnesses to the glorious past of Segesta. Probably the town was founded in prehistoric times, since it precedes the Phoenician and Greek colonizations. Virgil attributes it to the Trojan Aeneas. According to the ancient historians, the mysterious Elimi, who lived here, were of Trojan origin. We find Segesta again in historical times, when it had become Greek in its customs and the enemy of Selinunte, which threatened its supremacy. Since it was too weak to defend itself, the town sought the support of Athens, then that of Carthage. It was sacked by the Syracusan Agetocles, but flourished again during the first period of the Roman domination. Then it began to decline, till the devastations caused by the Vandals and the Saracens destroyed it definitively.

As we have said, of Segesta today remain only ruins spread here and there, and the Temple and the Theatre. The Temple, built on a rock, dominates the surrounding bare hills. It is one of the best examples of Doric architecture. It is elegant and imposing. It has 36 columns, six of which are frontal and support the two gables and the trabeation. The traditional cell of the god is missing. Some think that there must have been only one altar dedicated to the cult of a local deity. A few metres higher, on the top of Mt. Barbaro, is the Theatre. It is a large semicircle with a diameter of more than 60 metres, with a magnificent flight of steps divided into seven wedges and cut into the rock. Beyond it one can enjoy a wonderful view.

Trapani

The town, situated on the west coast of Sicily, lies along a strip of land stretching forwards into the sea, and on a narrow plain at the foot of Mt. Erice.

The town was first ruled by the Carthaginians, then by the Romans, Saracens and Normans. It keeps, however, few traces of its past, also because of the many air and naval bombings it suffered during the last war. Today Trapani looks like a modern town with a very efficient harbour.

Its artistic patrimony includes the church of St. Augustine, dating back to the 14th century, restored after the damage caused by bombardments and today used as a concert-hall; the 16th century Giudecca Palace; the Sanctuary of Our Lady of the Annunciation, the greatest monument in the town, dating back to the 14th century, but often restored and modified, as the Baroque belfry shows; the Pepoli National Museum, which keeps a good archaeological collection of Statues and paintings.

In order to know Trapani and its life adequately, it is necessary to visit the salt-works. Lastly you should reach Erice, the small town situated on the top of the homonymous mountain. From here you can enjoy a wonderful view and, when the day is particularly clear, your eyes can sweep the landscape up to the African coasts.

The tourist who visits the town on Good Friday, should watch, by night, the procession of the «Mysteries», namely twenty wooden, life-size groups, which were sculpted in the 18th century, representing episodes of the Passion of Jesus.

Views of the port.

THE PEPOLI NATIONAL MUSEUM

This Museum is situated in the old Carmelite convent of Our Lady of the Annunciation, and keeps very important archaeological finds, sculptures and an important picture-gallery.

The collection of the works kept in this Museum was begun in 1827 by the municipality and went on to include various donations and the collection of Count Agostino Sieri Pepoli, who wanted it to be situated where it is now.

Since 1925 the Museum has belonged to the Italian State, which has seen to rearranging and restoring all the material.

The works occupy many halls, situated on the two floors of the building.

On the ground floor is the archaeological material found in Trapani and Erice, and 18th century sculptures, almost all made by Gagini. The upper floor is occupied by the picture-gallery, which includes works by Titian, Guarino, De Mura, Caracciolo, De Caro and many others. There is also the section of the minor arts, with products of Trapanese craftsmanship, the Hall of the prints, some of which were made by Rembrandt, the great Dutch painter of the 17th century, the archaeological section and an exhibition of ancient, medieval and modern coins, together with some Renaissance medals.

Erice

A populous little town clinging to the slopes of Monte San Giuliano - which was in fact its name until the early 20th century - Erice has a medieval town-plan of triangular shape, traversed by a series of silent alleys and characterized by houses dating to the 13th and 14th centuries. Already settled in ancient times and famous for its temple of Venus (said to have been founded by Aeneas), it was inhabited by the Phoenicians, the Greeks and the Romans. Later the Arabs occupied the town, followed by the Normans.

The townplan is of particular interest, due to its well-preserved medieval structure with architecture of various styles and influences, its medieval walls, which follow a triangular perimeter, and the presence of some notable ancient buildings. The latter include in particular the 14th century Mother Church, with a fine facade characterized by a portal with a pronounced pronaos and a bell-tower with two storeys of mullioned windows and merIons on top; it was converted out of an ancient guard-tower. Also worth visiting are the church of San Giovanni Battista, built in the 13th century but in part reconstructed, the ancient Pepoli Castle which occupies the site of the former temple of Venus Ericina, still in part visible on one side of the Fortress, now converted into a private residence.

The most interesting of the archaeological finds from the ancient city are displayed in the Civic Museum. They include a head of Venus.

The most significant remains of the medieval town include the already-mentioned town walls, which give a distinctive character to the town with their perfectly triangular perimeter and their often enormous blocks of ashlared masonry. The circuit of walls is attributable in part to the 7th-6th century B.C., i.e. the Greek period, and in part to the Normans.

Facing page, above: *The Turret of the Castle of Pepoli.*
Below: *The Temple of Venus Ericina.*
This page: *The Church of St. John the Baptist.*
Below: *View from the Temple of Venus Ericina.*

Selinunte

It was probably founded by Megara Hyblaea in 650 B.C. It was named after the wild parsley, which is quite widespread in this area and was called selinon by the Greeks. It was the most western of the Greek colonies and certainly one of the most flourishing, if we consider its beautiful and imposing monuments. It was destroyed by the Carthaginians in 409 B.C. and after two years restored by the Syracusan Ermocrates. In 250 B.C., however, it received its final blow, again from Carthage, when its inhabitants were compelled to seek refuge at Lilibeo. During the early Middle Ages hermits and religious communities lived here. In the Byzantine age a violent earthquake destroyed its wonderful monuments, and for centuries the ruins were used as materials to build the nearby country houses.

The town lay on a plain situated between two small valleys, and was divided into two parts connected by an isthmus. On the south side, stretching into the sea, was the oldest part of the town and the Acropolis, of which the A, B, C, D, and O temples remain. On the north side was the real town.

On another plain, to the east, were the magnificent Oriental Temples. They are three, namely G, F and E. Of them the G temple is the largest in Selinunte, and one of the biggest buildings of Greek architecture.

From an inscription discovered in 1871, we learn that probably it was dedicated to Apollo, the patron-god of the town. We do not know to which deities the other temples were dedicated; this is why they are indicated with letters of the alphabet.

At about 800 metres from the Acropolis, where the remains of great fortification works are, is the Sanctuary of Malophoros, where probably funerals stopped before reaching the necropolises of Manicalunga.

Above: *A view of Temple A.*
Below and on the following page: *Views of Temple C.*

Facing page: *Views of Temple E.*
This page, above: *View of Temple G.*
Below: *View of Temple E.*

The Egadi Island

From Trapani one can easily reach the archipelago of the Egadi, a group of three islands, Favignana, Levanzo and Maréttimo. They are particularly interesting thanks to the landscape, which is beautiful, but rough and steep as well. The islets of Formica and Maraone, very near the Sicilian coast, are part of the archipelago. If you go by boat around them, you can admire the clear outlines of the coasts, and get into the many sea caves with their enchanting and phantasmagoric atmosphere. The exceptional and impressing spectacle of the tunny-fishing is well worth seeing. It takes place during the months of May and June, mainly in Favignana and Formica. This kind of fishing takes place by stages, since it is necessary to prepare the nets, let them down some 30 metres below sea level, fasten them by anchors and floats, so as to form a set of rectangular rooms. All ends with the so called «mattanza» (killing), when the fish enter the last and more solid room, called the death-room, and are harpooned and hoisted onto the boats, which are all around the place. Fishing is the main resource of the inhabitants of these islands. Recently the Egadi Islands have become more important, thanks to the discovery, in some caves, of rupestrian engravings, dating back to the early palaeolithic age. Favignana, the largest of the Egadi, has the most important tunny-fishing nets in Sicily and tunny-working establishments. Maréttimo is the westernmost and most mountainous of the Egadi Islands. It has only one little town, whose inhabitants are for the most part engaged in farming. The Fort, now called Semaforo, that the Bourbons used as a prison, is still to be seen on the island. Innumerable caves exist along the coast. The finest of them, the Grotta del Presepe (Grotto of the Crib), is full of stalagmites. It was in the waters between

Maréttimo and Favignana that the Carthaginian fleet with Hanno at its head was defeated by the Roman fleet commanded by the consul L. Lutatius Catulus in 241 B.C. The small island of Lévanzo, only some 5 km. long and 2 km. wide, has very rocky coasts. Its only settlement has the same name as the island.

The island's interest is almost exclusively due to the existence of a number of caves (the Grotta Grande, Grotta dei Porci, Grotta Crollata and others), almost all of them of prehistoric interest.

Sciacca

This important bathing and thermal resort is situated on a terrace sloping down to the sea.

It has various monuments and works of art: Steripinto palace; the 12th century Cathedral, entirely remade in the 18th century, which keeps its three original apses and is adorned with statues made by Antonio and Gian Domenico Gagini. Then there is St. Margaret's church, with a side portal in Gothic-Renaissance style, made by Laurana.

The spa of the town exploits the curative waters of the hydrothermal basin of Sciacca.

A long flight of steps leads to C. Colombo promenade and to the harbour protected by a small dock.

Agrigento

This town, situated on a hill, with its narrow streets and steps, is very important from the artistic point of view. The reason is that near it there is an incomparably beautiful archaeological area - the famous Valley of the Temples. The ancient Akragas was founded by some Rhodian settlers of Gela in 581 B.C. It became so important, powerful and rich that Pindar called it the «most beautiful town of mortals». Many slaves worked on the construction of the monuments, of which today we can admire the remains.

In the 3rd century A.D., however, it began to decline.

The Valley of the Temples constitutes a very important and suggestive area from the architectonic point of view, with its wonderful temples of Juno Lacinia, Corcord, Hercules, Castor and Pollux, and Olympic Jupiter and the huge human figures called «telamons».

The Temples, situated in the middle of the countryside, are made of yellow-coloured conchiferous sandstone tuff. The nearby Archaeological Museum keeps the materials found in the area. This collection is very rich and shows the developments of the history and art of the Greek civilization in its colonies and how the colonies themselves knew how to become powerful and important by effectively exploiting all the elements from their mother-land.

Of the modern town, worth mentioning are only some medieval and Baroque remains, such as the Holy Spirit Abbey (13th century), the church of Holy Mary of the Greeks, so called because it was a cathedral of the Greek cult (13th century), and the Cathedral (13th century), with a belfry built later. The beauty of the town, its artistic patrimony and its mild climate make Agrigento a very important holiday resort and tourist centre.

Among the most renowned citizens of Agrigento we should mention the philosopher Empedocles (5th century B.C.), and, more recently, the novelist and playwright Luigi Pirandello (1867-1936).

THE TEMPLE OF CONCORD

Erected in the middle of the 5th century BC, it's almost intact in spite of the friability of the materials used for its construction. The deity, to whom it was dedicated, is unknown and it was named after a Latin inscription having no relation with this temple and discovered in the surroundings. It is a peripteral hexastyle, with 34 fluted pillars. Once it was covered by a polychrome stuccos.

THE TEMPLE OF JUNO OR HERA LACINIA

Erected in 460-440 B.C., the temple stands on the top of the hill of the temples, in a very happy position, from which it dominates the valley below, down to the sea, and, upwards, the Rupe Atenea. It is wrongly called «Temple of Hera», confusing it with the real Temple of Hera situated on the Lacinio promontory in Crotone. Of the 34 original pillars, 25 are still standing: more than nine pillars are mutilated. Though smaller, it has forms like those of the Temple of Concord. Traces of the fire Akragas suffered in 406 B.C. by the Carthaginians can still be seen on the reddish blocks of the cell.

THE TEMPLE OF HERCULES

Erected in a very suggestive scenographic position, above the last stretch of the way of the temples, the Temple of Hercules is thought to be the most ancient one, belonging to the end of the 6th century B.C. It is a peripteral hexastyle (6 X 15 pillars) and the only one still keeping a certain archaic flavour in the remarkably large ptera (side pillars), in the curved lines of capitals and pillars and in the noticeably long plan (74 X 28 metres). Belonging to the golden age of Greek archaism, it was adorned with facings, statues and paintings. Out of the original 38 pillars, only 8 are still standing, of which only four with their capitals.

TEMPLE OF CASTOR AND POLLUX OR THE DIOSCURI

Erected during the 5th century BC, it has a very ornate and complex trabeation, which is certainly Hellenistic. The temple, however, must have been restored later in its higher parts, having been seriously damaged when the town was taken and ransacked by the Carthaginians in 406 B.C.

THE CAVEA OR «EKKLESIASTIRION»

It is a sort of a theatrical area, dug in the rock, belonging to the republican Roman period of the 3rd century BC. What probably was a cavea for assemblies, is now the only preserved civil building of ancient Agrigento.
In the background is the so called «Oratorio di Falaride», which once was thought to be the monumental tomb of a Roman matron of the 1st century BC. It is, however, a small temple rising on a rectangular podium of that period, belonging to a sanctuary once situated here. In the Middle Ages it was transformed into a chapel.

THE TEMPLE OF AESCULAPIUS

The Temple of Aesculapius whose remains were brought to light in 1926, is situated on the banks of the river Akragas, in the plain sloping down towards the sea, to the south of the Valley of the Temples. It is a small temple in antis with a pseudo-portico, perhaps of the 5th century BC. It included the famous statue of Apollo, a work of Nero, stolen by the Carthaginian Imilcon, recuperated by Scipio and then stolen by Verres.

The Temple of Castor and Pollux.

THE TEMPLE OF OLYMPIAN ZEUS

The temple is dedicated to Zeus, father of all the gods and lord of Olympus. For this reason it is also known as the "Olympieion". It survives as a gigantic scatter of ruins, which immediately suggests that it must have been of colossal dimensions. In fact it measured some 113 metres in length and 56.30 in width. In spite of the fact that only the structures of the podium and a few other architectural elements remain visible to this day, the impression one gets from these ruins is one of imposing grandeur and awesome monumentality. Indeed, in terms of mere size, it was the third biggest religious building of antiquity. Erected between 480 and 470 B.C., immediately after the victory of Himera - a victory that marked the period of maximum splendor of ancient Agrigento - the temple represents, in architectural terms, an undoubtedly innovative experience. This is apparent not only as regards the building's structural form (it is in fact a pseudo - peripteral temple, which means that its exterior colonnading did not follow, as was usual in this type of sanctuary, the whole perimeter of the temple; instead, the columns along one side of the building were replaced

by a wall articulated by engaged half-columns). But the temple is also innovative for its method of construction, for example the practice of deriving some elements of the building from a single block of material in order to facilitate their putting into place. Yet the most striking feature of the Temple of Zeus are its colossal "Telamones": the huge caryatids or columns in the form of a male figure, which were used to support the entablature. They are some 8 metres in height (one is preserved in the Regional Archaeological Museum, while a copy of it can be seen recumbent on the ground by the Temple in all its length). These figures represent an extraordinary testimony to the creativeness of the architects of the temple. They also attest to their ability to devise original architectural solutions aimed at increasing the stability of the building which, in view of its exceptional size, might otherwise have posed problems of static equilibrium. These enormous figures were in fact incorporated in the interspace between the columns and served to support the lateral entablatures. The interior of the Temple of Zeus consisted of a double row of pillars which divided it into three aisles. The cella, or inner sanctuary of the god, was also tripartite in structure. The decorations of the Sactuary, unfortunately now lost, included - as we are told by the ancient historians - a pedimental sculptural representation of the "Battle of the Giants" and the "Trojan War".

THE REGIONAL ARCHAEOLOGICAL MUSEUM

Before leaving Agrigento, one should visit the Archaeological Museum, situated in the Town Hall Square, in a modern building, which includes what remains of the ancient monastery of St. Nicholas. The Museum, which is the largest one in middle-southern Sicily, keeps works dating back from the prehistoric age to the Hellenistic and Roman ages, and paintings dating back from the 14th to the 18th centuries. Most of the material kept in this Museum comes from Agrigento, the rest from the areas of the provinces of Agrigento and Caltanissetta. In the 19 halls forming the Museum there are, among others, a rich collection of vases; prehistoric materials dating back to the first and second millennium B.C., from ancient Akragas; a huge telamon, more than 7 metres high from the temple of

Olympic Jupiter; an epigraphic collection; a collection of Greek, Roman, Byzantine, Arab, Norman, bronze, silver and golden coins; two topographic sections of the provinces of Caltanisetta and Agrigento.

Luigi Pirandello

An illustrious son of Sicily, Luigi Pirandello was born at Girgenti (Agrigento) in 1867. His works have left their mark on an entire epoch, and on the literature of the first half of this century, with their well-defined character and great originality.

Apart from novels and essays, he also wrote stage-plays, for which he is now best remembered. Among his most famous plays are "Six Personages in Search of an Author" and "Henry IV", which remain among the most significant achievements of the Italian theatre and have had a major influence on world literature. Pirandello was honored for his literary achievements.

He was not only nominated Academician of Italy, but also awarded the Nobel Prize for Literature in 1934.

His output is shot through by a dark vein of pessimism and the existential anguish which pervaded the whole period. Each man, for Pirandello, wears a mask in front of his fellow-men and society: a mask which he involuntarily ends up by resembling.

Appearance and reality thus become fused. Man seems to lose his own identity, in the search for a reality that eludes him.

Lampedusa

Lampedusa, the «Lopadusa» of the Latins, is the largest and most important one of the Pelagie islands. Situated 113 kilometers away from the coasts of Tunisia and 205 kilometers from Sicily, Lampedusa is washed by the «African sea» and under its influence, the climate here is mild and constant all year long. Its northern steep coasts present incomparable natural beauties, with bays and caves, whose waters constitute a real paradise for underwater fishers. They abound in «cernie», hidden in green underwater caves, in golden maids, umbrinas and mullets.

On the less steep, south-east side, the coast mildly slopes down to the sea, where there are uncontaminated beaches with white velvet sand.

On the island there are traces of Phoenician, Greek, Roman and Arabian inhabitants, but only towards the middle of the 19th century did it begin to be colonized, by Ferdinand II of Bourbon.

Apart from the good port, it has an airport, too, which links it with Trapani and Palermo.

The main activities of the people are the fishing of sponges, which are exported all over the world and the fish packaging industry with many factories.

Piazza Armerina

It is situated on a hillock, in one of the most beautiful areas of Sicily, rich in woods, fruit-groves and olive-groves. It is the most important town of the province, apart from Enna.

The imposing structure of the Cathedral dominates the entire built-up area.

It was begun by Orazio Torriani in 1627. The building presents a large Baroque facade, a portal with twisted columns and a bell-tower. The latter was built for a pre-existing church and keeps in its lower part the Gothic-Catalan style. In the upper one, built later, it has a 16th century look.

In the interior, in the chapel to the left of the presbytery, there is an exceptional Crucifix by an unknown author, painted on wood, on both sides.

On the main altar there is a Byzantine-like Madonna, which, according to tradition, was donated in 1509 by Pope Nicholas II to Count Roger the Norman, as a good omen for the deliverance of Sicily from the Saracens.

Worth seeing are also the 14th century Spinelli Castle, the Baroque church of St. Peter and that of St. Andrew (built in 1096), where some frescoes dating back to the 12th, 13th and 15th centuries have been found.

Today they are kept in the National Gallery of Palermo.

Piazza Armerina is particularly interesting thanks to the remains of the magnificent Roman Villa of Casale about 6 kilometres from the town. This villa, built between the 3th and 4th century A.D., was often delivered between 1930 and 1960 from the mud which during the 12th century had covered and at the same time protected it from the destroying action of atmospheric agents. Today it is still the largest Roman construction in Sicily and one of the greatest in ancient times. Now the villa, without its original covering, is protected by a plastic covering.

In its interior there are some very

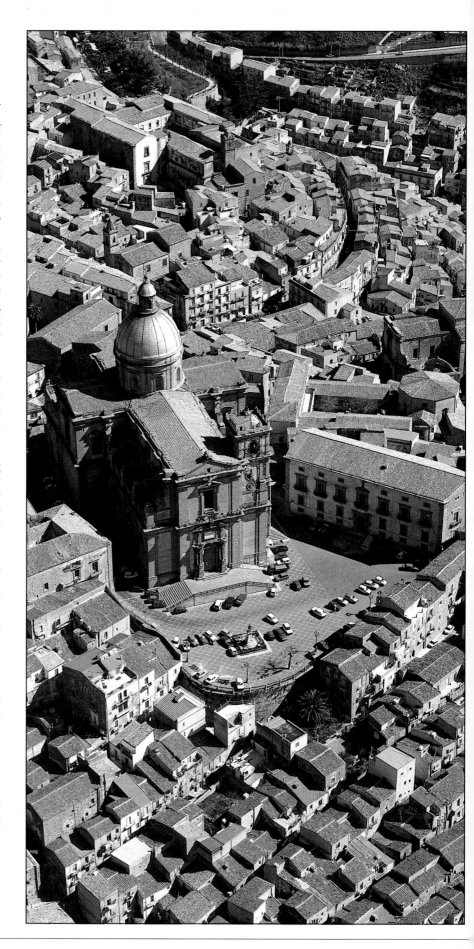

interesting mosaics on the floor. The wonderful Villa of Casale is very large. It includes a courtyard, baths with a frigidarium and calidarium, a vestibule, a large rectangular peristyle and an elliptic one, a large hall with an apse, a triclinium with three apses and several bedrooms. Mosaics cover almost all the area of the villa (more than 3500 square metres) and present various subjects. In the ambulatory the mosaics, for 60 metres, represent hunting scenes, in which men armed with spears and shields try to capture, without killing them, some wild animals, which are later embarked in the presence of a high imperial officer. On the right side, in the centre of the mosaic of the eastern apse of the triclinium, there is the image of the giant, who struck to death by Hercule's arrow, vainly tries to take it out of his breast. In the so called «Small-game hunting Hall» the scene of the country sacrifice to Diana and that of the banquet under the trees during a hunting party are particularly interesting. The mosaic, which covers the floor of one of the rooms to the south of the large peristyle, represents 10 girls wearing dresses similar to bathing-suits («bikinis»). There is also a teacher giving prizes to girls taking part in various competitions. This mosaic is posterior to the others, since it was placed on a more ancient one with a geometric design. A Homer-inspired mosaic, which is in the vestibule of one of the private apartments, represents the giant Polyphemus sitting on a rock under the arch of rocks delimiting his den, with a killed ram on his knees. Before him is Ulysses, who offers him a cup of wine, while his companions fill another one in order to make him drunk.

The mosaics of the villa are some of the best examples of Roman art in this field. Many artists worked on them. They knew how to reproduce with realism and psychological vigour mythical scenes and also scenes reflecting life at that time. The magnificence and splendour of the whole building lead us to think that it was a hunting resort of the Emperor Maximian Herculean. It was undoubtedly built by order of a very rich man.

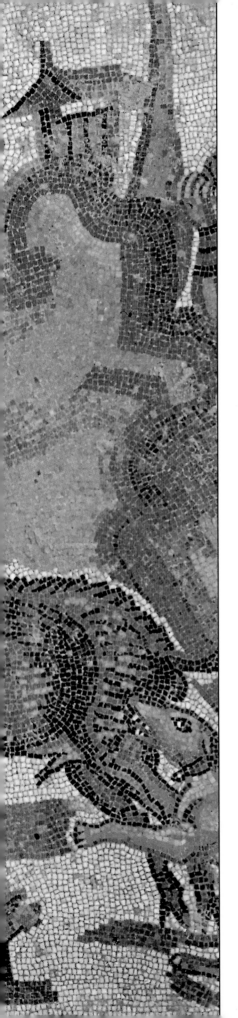

Morgantina

This Greek town, founded in the 5th century B.C., was probably situated along a road, which from Leontini led to Enna. Thanks to its situation, Morgantina was a very important centre during the Hellenistic and Roman ages. According to the historical sources, the town was called after the mythical king of the Morgeti, an Italian tribe, settled here in protohistorical times. According to a recent supposition, the ancient Morgantina is the settlement discovered near Serra Orlando by an American expedition. It consists of imposing ruins, among which there are the remains of a «bouleterium» and the theatre, the remains of stores, many terraced houses and a shrine dedicated to Demetra and Kores, dating back probably to the 6th century. As a matter of fact, it is still impossible to identify the town with absolute certainty. Because of its topographical situation, this town could have been a place under the influence of Gela, or could be the ancient Licodia Eubea of Caltagirone, since we know that Syracuse and Camarina contended for it.

Enna

It is the highest main town of a province in Italy, since it lies on a hill at 948 metres above sea level. It is also the most central town in Sicily, so as to have been called by Callimachus the «navel of Sicily». Enna is an ancient Sicilian town ruled successively by Carthaginians, Romans, Byzantines and Normans. It was very dear to Frederick II of Swabia and Frederick II of Aragon. In the highest part of the town, from where one can enjoy a wonderful view, rises the Castle of Lombardy, one of the most interesting medieval castles in Sicily. It was built in a strategic situation dominating the whole gorge below.

In order to make it even safer, the slopes of the mountain were partly cut to prevent enemies from climbing up. In its inside courtyards there is now an open theatre with 8000 seats. From the top of a hill, in a situation

different from that of the Castle, the octagonal Tower of Frederick II of Swabia, 24 metres high, dominates the whole area. One should also visit the Alessi Museum, which keeps a precious collection of Greek-Sicilian and Roman coins, ceramics, prints and paintings; and the Cathedral, of which we'll speak later.

From Enna one can easily reach the lake of Pergusa, with a surface of little more than 5 square kilometres. This lake, which is only 4 metres deep, and surrounded by eucalyptus, is used for hunting-parties with boats, motor-boat competitions and water-skiing. An autodrome for international competitions runs along its perimeter. According to a mythological story, it was here that Pluto abducted Proserpine. It is also very interesting to visit Calascibetta, a picturesque small town a few kilometres from Enna.

View of the Duomo (cathedral) and of the Lombardia Castle.

Ragusa

The town consists of two parts - Ragusa, which is the modern one and Ragusa Ibla, full of old buildings, since it is the ancient one.

Only since 1926 have the two parts united to form one town,and in the following year it became the main town of the province. In Ragusa Ibla many are the testimonies of the past, among which the basilica of St. George (18th century) and the church of St. Joseph (16th century), both planned by Rosario Gagliardi with a Baroque facade crowned above by the bell-tower, a characteristic of his architecture. In the new town one can see the Baroque Cathedral and the Archaeological Museum, which keeps the material found in Ragusa and in the areas of the province. In it are kept the remains of built-up areas dating back to the 6th, 4th and 3rd centuries, and a factory of ceramics with its kiln, clay vases and the tools used to make them, has been reconstructed. Today Ragusa is mainly an industrial town, thanks to the asphalt mines, the most important ones in the world, and some plants which produce hydraulic limes and cements.

Around 1950, drilling in the ground of Ragusa's environs led to the discovery of oil and to the construction of a pipeline which takes the crude oil up to the refineries of Augusta.

Modica

The town lies in the place of the ancient Motyka, partly on a hillock and partly in the plain.

St. George's church superbly rising on a flight of 250 steps, is very beautiful and suggestive. It was built in the first half of the 18th century by Rosario Gagliardi. Its central part is quite round and rises like a spire to form the bell-tower. Five portals lead into the interior, where, in a silver urn, St. George's relics are kept (18th century).

The church of Holy Mary of Bethlehem, built in the 15th century, but later entirely re-built.

In its interior one can see the Chapel of the Sacrament, an example of late-Gothic-Renaissance architecture, which opens with a richly decorated ogival arch, on a square plan surmounted by a dome.

From the square before the church one can see the Castle above. We advise you to reach, from here, Ispica's quarry, the valley hollowed out by the homonymous river for 10 kilometres, in the calcareous tableland of the Iblei mountains. In the quarry there are traces of the presence of man from the copper age almost to the present - Siculian necropolises, Christian catacombs, primitive houses.

Noto

This town, entirely re-built after it was destroyed by an earthquake in 1693, presents an 18th century look, harmonious and superb as it is. The Civic Museum is very important.

It has an archaeological section, whose materials come mainly from the area of Noto, and a modern section, which keeps relics of the Italian «Risorgimento» and the projects of the architects, who built the new Noto.

Monuments which are worth seeing: the church of the Most Holy Crucifix, the Cathedral, the Bishop's House, the Town Hall, with a portico on the ground floor and a balcony on the first floor, and the church of St. Dominic, in which the typical architecture of its author, Rosario Gagliardi, is quite evident. In the church there is a Madonna of the Rosary (1703), probably made by Vito d'Anna and a 17th century lavabo.

Views of the Duomo (above) and of the Church of the Sacred Crucifix.

Siracusa

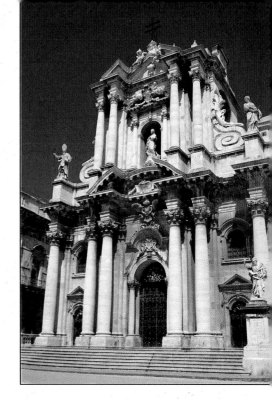

Ortygia island with its ruins of primitive circular huts, was the original nucleus on which Syracuse was subsequently founded by the Corinthians in the 8th century B.C.. It developed so rapidly that just 70 years later its inhabitants founded 3 colonies: Akrai, Kasmenai and Kamarina.

In the 6th century the city was governed by the Gamorroi after they had subjugated and deprived of all their political rights the Cirilli, who, however, after a revolt, succeeded in putting them to flight. The Gamorroi sought help from Gelon, the tyrant of Gela, who occupied the city, destroyed its rival Kamarina, transferred his court to Syracuse uniting the territory with that of Gela and built arsenals which allowed Syracuse to become a strong naval power. So aware of this were the tyrants who governed the city subsequently, exploiting this characteristic to wage war with the Etruscans, the Lentini and their Athenian allies - roundly defeating them on two occasions - that the latter renounced their expansionist designs on the Mediterranean. It is to this period that the legislation of Dion dates, a code of written laws and constitutional reforms including the election of magistrates by the drawing of lots, of typically Athenian character.

As a result of the banishment of the former, Syracuse was attacked by the Carthaginians with whom Dionysius I - having had himself elected plenipotentiary - stipulated a peace treaty in which it was established that Carthage would assume control of Western Sicily and the Greek cities of Selinus, Akragas, Himera, Gela and Kamarina and that Dionysius would take on the role of tyrant of Syracuse. During this period Dionysius commissioned the building of the Eurialo Castle in further defence of the city. A period of internal conflict followed which Agathocles put an end to by taking the title of basileus (king).

After his reign, the Cathaginians threatened Syracuse once more and it was in the midst of this predicament that Hiero II seized power. He put to flight the Mamertines and negotiated peace with the Romans: the peace lasted for 50 years until such time as the Roman Consul Marcellus conquered the city.

Later on it came under the sway of the succession of invaders who overran the island: it was sacked by the Franks, conquered by the Goths and the Byzantines, who made it the Capital of the Eastern Empire, by the Arabs, the Normans, who restored it to its ancient splendour, and by the Swabians. This was the situation up until the great earthquake of 1693 which virtually destroyed the city: it was rebuilt entirely in the Baroque style. After 1860, the year of Italian unity, the Umbertine district was built on the mainland and the walls built by the Spaniards knocked down: the present-day city is a harmonious mix of ancient vestiges and modern features.

View of the Duomo and of the oceanfront at Siracusa (Isle of Ortigia).

The Greek Theatre and the Grotto of the Nymphaeum

Amidst the grandeur of the statues of the Dioscuri on Horseback and the dynamic majesty of Triptolemus portrayed on a chariot pulled by serpents, by way of Via dei Sepolcri, we reach the top of Temenite Hill.

On its terrace lies the wonder of Syracuse: the Greek Theatre.

Dug out of the rock, it is laid out according to Greek architectural canons: cavea, orchestra and stage.

The cavea, 139 m in diameter, is made up of a semicircle of tiered steps where the public would sit, 46 of which, divided into 9 sections, are still visible today. The orchestra, a circular space between the stage and the steps, was intended for dances and for the chorus, whilst all that now remains of the stage are numerous cavities whose function is difficult to interpret.

The "maximum" theatre, as Cicero was wont to define it, was used both for performances pertaining to the Greek world, such as tragedies, and, after the necessary structural modifications were carried out, for events pertaining to the Roman world: gladiatorial games, combat with wild beasts and the like.

There is a small artificial grotto in the middle of the Temenite terrace, known as the "Grotto of the Nymphaeum".

It has a vaulted ceiling and inside houses a rectangular basin in the centre of which gushes a small cascade generated by a branch of the Greek aqueduct.

The Grotto of the Nymphaeum is now completely bare but in antiquity was decorated with statues representing the muses: some of these statues can now be found at the Regional Archaeological Museum of Syracuse.

QUARRY OF PARADISE

The "Latomie" are the ancient quarries from which the Greeks extracted stone for the building of roads, temples and for consolidation and defence works.

The extraction of material was carried out by prisoners condemned to this task: as well as being mining quarries they were used as actual prisons.

The "Quarry of Paradise" is at present only partially visible since it is still undergoing the consolidation work made necessary by the ancient mining system; this drove down so deep that, naturally, the effect of the earth movements generated over the years led first to the weakening and subsequently to the collapse of the caves on the outer edges of the Quarry.

Amidst the huge boulders bearing witness to past collapses, is the most famous of the caves in the Quarry of Paradise.

THE EAR OF DIONYSIUS

This funnel-shaped artificial grotto resembling an auricle was given its name by Caravaggio both because of its highly unusual shape and because of its incredible acoustic qualities, which allowed even the most modest sound to be naturally amplified to a truly remarkable degree. Legend has it that the tyrant Dionysius had this cave built as a prison and that his prisoners were shut up in there so the tyrant might overhear their conversations from an opening cut out at the top.

ROMAN AMPHITHEATRE

A grandiose construction of the 3rd or 4th century A.D., elliptical in shape, the amphitheatre was freed of the rubble and earth which buried it and brought to light in 1893. The lower part is dug out of the living rock, whilst the upper part was built in elevation. In the middle of the arena is a basin into which two channels flow.

PAOLO ORSI REGIONAL ARCHAEOLOGICAL MUSEUM

The Villa Landolina houses the Paolo Orsi Regional Archaeological Museum, a marvel of modern design.
It is one of the most important structures of its kind in Italy since it contains not only exhibits relating to prehistoric and protohistoric Sicilian civilisation, but extremely interesting Greek and Roman collections as well.
Divided into thematic areas - geology, palaeontology, Sicilian prehistory, the Doric and Ionic Hellenistic world, the Roman era - it houses numerous treasures, outstanding among which is the Venus Anadyomene (known as the Landolina Venus after the archaeologist who discovered it in Syracuse), a 2nd century B.C. marble statue of the Roman age with a Hellenistic subject.
Other first-rate exhibits include Kore - a female bust of the 4th century B.C. -, two equestrian statues - one of which used to adorn the Temple of Kamarina, and the other, made of limestone and representing a "mother god", originates from the necropolis of Megara Hyblaea -, the Small Bronze of the Offering Athlete which can be dated to around 460 B.C. and the numerous ceramics and funeral ornaments found at Thapsos.

Side: *Landolina Venus.*
Above: *Corinthian Lion 7th century B.C..*
Below: *Silver coins of Syracuse.*

THE GROTTO OF THE CORDARI

An ancient stone quarry, with truly extraordinary features.

ALTAR OF HIERO

This is the largest altar of the Greek age in existence.
Rectangular in shape and built by Hiero II for public sacrifices, it is thought that the altar may have been used for the sacrifice of more than 400 bulls.
Today, all that remains visible of the immense sacrificial altar is the base dug into the rock, since the upper part was destroyed by the Spaniards after 1700.

THE CHURCH OF ST. JOHN THE EVANGELIST

Now in ruins, it is very old. The building consists of a portico, built with the remains of a pre-existing construction; a facade with a very fine portal, and the remains of the Doric columns of the nave.

THE FOUNTAIN OF ARETHUSA

We could describe the spring of fresh water which gushes out from a grotto a few metres from the sea with reference to the choreographic presence of the papyrus submerged in it, or Pindar, Virgil and D'Annunzio who celebrated it, or Cicero who mentions it in his "Verrines"; but it is perhaps the love affair between the nymph Arethusa and the god Alpheus which best explains the interest in this myth which has fascinated men in every age. Arethusa, a handmaid of Artemis, was glimpsed by the river god Alpheus: he fell in love with her and in a fit of passion tried to seduce her against her will.

The nymph then fled and was turned into a fountain near Ortygia by Artemis.

Moved to pity by Alphaeus' pain, Zeus turned him into a river, thus allowing him to join his waters with those of the fountain.

Arethusa, always close to the hearts of the people of Syracuse, was depicted on more than one occasion in the stamps on their splendid coins: from her flowing locks leap fish and dolphins.

EURIALO CASTLE

About 8 km. from the city situated in the Epipoli, or "high part" of Syracuse, stands the most ingenious work of the Hellenistic world.

The Eurialo Castle has a surface area of abut 15,000 sq. m., trenches, a drawbridge, moats and lookout towers which made the city truly impregnable.

The castle was built at the behest of Dionysius I in the period in which Syracuse was at war with Carthage: it took the work of 65,000 men to make possible in just six days the construction of a five-kilometre-long wall. The rest of the fortress was built in the following years.

Subsequently, at the height of the Byzantine epoch, it was modified as a result of the Arab threat to the city. From the top of the Epipoli it is possible to catch a glimpse of Mount Etna.

SANCTUARY OF THE MADONNA OF THE TEARS

This impressive, futuristic sanctuary is the work of the French architects Parat and Andraud.

The upper church has a surface area of around 4,700 sq. m. and the height of the construction is well over 74 metres.

On its top rises a 20-metre-high steel structure, supporting a gilded bronze statue depicting the Madonna, which is thus made visible to pilgrims even at a distance.

In the circular crypt 18 entrances have been "dug out" and 12 chapels "sculpted": it has a maximum diameter of 80 metres and can hold up to 3,000 worshippers.

The upper church, where a gigantic Christ on the cross is suspended above the altar, is a place of prayer and meditation for around 10,000 of the faithful. The Sanctuary was built in commemoration of a plaster moulding representing the heart of Mary which wept tears: this event took place on 29th August 1953 at the home of two humble workmen.

Pilgrims flocked there in growing numbers from neighbouring areas, then from all over Italy, until the present day when it has become a destination for pilgrims worldwide.

RIVER ANAPO

It is the best known of the rivers which flow towards the Ionian coast, thanks to the original landscape surrounding it and the battles which took place along its shores. Having crossed the narrow gorge of Pantalica, from where it is possible to reach the tombs of the largest Sicilian necropolis, the Anapo flows into the «Porto Grande» of Syracuse.

ROMAN GYMNASIUM

This vast Roman complex, including a theatre, a quadriporticus and a temple, perhaps dates back to the second half of the 1st century A.D..

Temple of Apollo.
Below: *Roman Gymnasium.*

Catania

Almost at the end of this journey in Sicily, on the slopes of Mt. Etna, the volcano which with its conical structure and clear outline dominates it, is the great and wonderful Catania, the largest Sicilian town, apart from Palermo. It was a Chalcidian colony, which became so important it was enriched with temples, a theatre, gymnasium, acqueducts, baths, a mint and treasury. Then it was ruled by the Romans, Goths, Byzantines, Saracens, Normans, Spaniards and Bourbons. In 1860 it was annexed to the Kingdom of Italy.

Catania has often been afflicted by pestilence, eruptions of Mt. Etna and by earthquakes, but each time it rose again, even more beautiful than before. Today it is a modern and active town, whose economic life depends mainly on the harbour, where trade flourishes, and on prosperous industries.

The artistic patrimony of the town consists of some renowned works, such as the Cathedral, whose apse dates back to the 11th-12th century; Ursino Castle, built by order of Frederick II in the 13th century; the church of S. Agatha, and the Collegiate church, both dating back to the 18th century; some palaces, museums; some ancient buildings, such as the Theatre, the Amphitheatre and the Odeon. In order to know Catania even better, one should walk along the central Etnea Street, and mainly the beautiful Via dei Crociferi, flanked with wonderful 18th century buildings. The town is also a very frequented bathing resort, thanks to the beautiful beach, provided with many sports and tourist plants, which make the stay very pleasant.

Once one has visited Catania, one can climb Mt. Etna, where we can enjoy one of the most exciting and suggestive spectacles.

BELLINI THEATRE

It is one of the most important Opera Houses in Italy, dedicated to the great musician of Catania.

It was built at the end of the 19th century by Andrea Scala and Carlo Sada. It has a rich facade, a large staircase with a gallery, four orders of boxes, and a ceiling richly decorated with an «Apotheosis of Bellini» by Ernesto Bellandi.

THE CATHEDRAL

On the east side of the harmonious Cathedral Square, with the Elephant's Fountain in the centre, within a marble enclosure adorned with statues, is the Cathedral, built in 1092 and rebuilt once in 1169. After the earthquake which took place in 1693, the church was completely rebuilt to designs by G. Palazzotto. From 1730 to 1736 G. B. Vaccarini built the sumptuous facade with two orders of columns, adorned, above, with a niche with the statues of St. Agatha and an Angel, and the left side, obtaining highly scenographic but also stylistically perfect effects. Of the original construction remain the transept, with two unfinished towers on its sides, and three semi-circular apses with simple arches of the Arab type. In the magnificent interior, too, with a nave and two aisles, recent restoration works have brought to light many elements of the old structure, hidden under the 18th century facing.

THE URSINO CASTLE

The Ursino Castle was built in 1239, by order of Frederick II of Swabia, by the architect Riccardo da Lentini, who took twelve years, and was used as a fortress on the sea-shore. From the end of the 13th century to the times of Alfonso d'Aragona (1520) it was the house of the Aragonese family. Later it became the residence of the Viceroys. After the splendour of the 16th century, an age of decline followed and so this castle became successively a military quarter and prison. In 1836 the Municipality gave it to the Bourbons. Having been neglected for a long time, it was used as military barracks, till 1915 when it housed Austrian prisoners. Only in 1932 was it completely restored on the initiative of the great writer Federico De Roberto. Though it has not been restored to its old magnificence because of numberless despoliations, it has again the dignity of a monument. In the interior, where the municipal museum is, one can admire many archaeological pieces, paintings and the rare private collection of Biscari.

THE VALLEY OF ALCANTARA

The deep furrow cut through the centuries by the homonymous river between the ranges of the Nebrodi-Peloritani Mountains and the massif of Etna, is very important, not only because of the wonderful landscape it offers and its role in the economy of the island, but also because of the historical events with which it has been associated.

It has been the natural way the invaders of Sicily have always taken, and, as a matter of fact, all those who from the Ionian Sea want to reach the centre of the island have to take. The reason is that this valley, in its higher part, meets the Valley of the Simeto and then the Valley of the Salso, which leads to Enna.

But it is no less interesting in terms of its landscape. Climbing up the slopes of the Nebrodi Mountains, our eyes sweep the deep and green valley up to Mt. Tauro and Schisò Cape, with a panorama of fertile hills sloping sweetly down, with the various shades of green of the intensive agriculture.

While enjoying the landscape, one recalls the many historical events associated with the names of places: the Byzantine Maniace, the Latin Mojo, the Arab Kaggi, Motta Camastra, Calatabiano and Castiglione and Francavilla, where the river-bed falls into a deep furrow cut through the centuries by the waters of the Alcantara, which have created a unique phenomenon of uncommon beauty in the Gorges of Larderia.

Etna

Sicily has in store for us now another of its wonders. Mt. Etna, the greatest active volcano in Europe.

We are before a magnificent and exceptional spectacle, which cannot but arouse our enthusiasm much more than the volcanoes of the Aeolian Islands. The activity of this volcano has been known since antiquity, so much so that it was thought to be Vulcan's and Cyclops' forge. Eruptions have followed one another, with more or less violence, till the last one, which took place in 1950-51.

The composition of the ancient lava' is different from that of the modern one, but it is always rich in the potassium oxide and phosphorus anhydride which make this area so fertile.

On its sides, covered with fertile deposits, vines, olive-trees, almond trees and citrus fruits grow up to 1000 metres; then there are woods up to 2000 metres. Above that, the landscape becomes lunar with heaps of lava and ashes everywhere. There are a crater and 250 cones, out of which white-hot material flows every now and then. Near the top there is the terminal crater (with a circumference of 3 kilometres and 200 metres in depth), which is mainly an orifice for gas leakage. By a cableway one can reach a height of 2935 metres in 20 minutes, the area where the Volcanological Observatory is. Then one can go on foot up to the crater, with its exceptional and terrifying look.

Expert guides take the tourists to see the huge mouth - we advise you to visit it by night, because you can see the lava bubbling at the bottom - and the large cracks in the ground, where the temperature is very high.

It is wonderful to watch the sun rising, lighting up the top of the mountain, then the whole area below and the Straits, the coast of Calabria up to Aspromonte, the Aeolian Islands, Syracuse, the rock of Acicastello.

Taormina

All this has made this town a renowned holiday resort, the charming and elegant residence of many people of the so called «jet-set», a must for all those who visit Sicily.

The town, situated on the sides of Mt. Tauro, can be reached by a winding and picturesque road, the Pirandello Road, which offers characteristic and pleasant sights.

The ancient Tauromenion - this was once its name - was inhabited by the Siculans, then became an allied town and later a colony of the Romans.

It flourished especially during the Middle Ages, but afterwards immediately declined. The acropolis of the town was situated on the top of Mt. Tauro and the built-up area along the north-east side, where today are the remains of the Greek Theatre, the Odeon, a Roman construction, dating back to the imperial age, found in 1893 and of the Naumachia, a magnificent Roman work, consisting of a terracing of the hill, to protect a huge tank. Worth seeing are also the baths dating back to the Roman Imperial age; the Ciampoli and Corvaia Palaces, both dating back to the 15th century: the 13th century Cathedral, later modified; and the Palace of the Dukes of St. Stephen, an elegant building and fine example of 14th and 15th century Sicilian architecture. The beauties of Taormina, however, are not found only in its monuments and palaces, but also in every corner, street and terrace, in the picturesque and elegant look of its houses, in its luxuriant vegetation, in its beautiful and clear sea.

St. Dominic's Hotel

The convent of St. Dominic, deconsecrated and since 1895 transformed into a hotel, lies in a fine position. It looks quite plain on the otuside, but it houses a first class hotel.

Piazza IX Aprile

This square looks like a large panoramic terrace with a wide view of the town, the theatre and the coast; Etna, too, is visible.

At the end of Ninth of April Square we notice the clock-tower. To the right is the belfry of the church of St. Joseph in Baroque style, of which we can clearly see the bell-portico, on which the pyramidal spire rests. The belfry is completely separated from the church, also built in Baroque style with characteristic undulating skews.

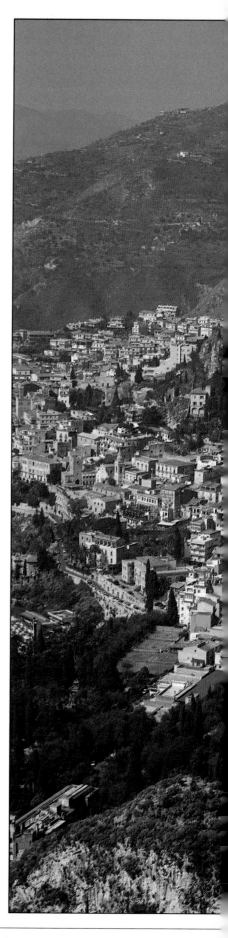

Piazza IX Aprile.

THE CATHEDRAL (ST. NICHOLAS)

Built in the 13th century over a church which already existed, it was rebuilt during the 15th and 16th centuries and modified in the 18th century. Externally the squared-off severe lines recall those of the Norman cathedrals. The façade has a portal dated 1636, flanked by two ogival windows with one light, above which is a small rose-window with delicate 16th century decorations. Inside, the aisle and two naves are set apart by two rows of monolithic marble pillars which support pointed arches. The aisle and transept have wooden trussed ceilings supported by shelves with arabesque-type carvings. The vestry houses a precious collection of gold jewellery of various periods.

THE GREEK THEATRE

The theatre is a masterpiece of Greek art: of an art which achieved forms as highly evolved as the religious and philosophical thought that the Greeks exported to the shores of southern Italy, and that heralded, through supreme and definitive figurative forms, the foundation of a new artistic, civil and cultural heritage.

The Greek theatre is the result of the translation into figurative language of the exquisite conceptions of thought taught by the immortal masters Phidias, Skopas, Praxiteles and Lysippos.

In the theatre, too, we find a reflection of the canons of perfection, of the immortal and immaculate idea of beauty, of the mystical serenity far removed from the overpowering passions of daily life, so dear to Greek artists. Here, therefore, at Taormina, at the source of the new civilization, we find an expression of the flourishing culture of ancient Greece: a theatre to whose perfection of form two factors contributed in perfect tandem: the search for aesthetic beauty, and the search for functional form. It is situated on a slope above the town, whence the spectator can enjoy an extensive panoramic view embracing in a single sweep the Greek architecture itself, the natural landscape, the shoreline of the bay and the austere forms of Mount Etna. The panorama is visible in an optimal way from the terraces situated to the sides of the scenic wall and from the top of the auditorium, from where a wonderful view can be enjoyed through the ruins of the stage in front.

The theatre's exceptional acoustics, its delightful situation and the atmosphere created by its ancient structures, form the essential ingredients for enhancing the high quality theatrical performances that are still staged here today.

The original Greek building of the theatre dates to the 3rd century B.C. Under the Romans, however, a number of alterations were made to it in the 2nd century A.D.: especially at the expense of the upper part of the auditorium and the stage. These underwent considerable changes. The front was displaced towards the orchestra (i.e. the semicircular space in front of the stage) and embellished with columns. The stage changed appearance as a result of the erection of the portico that delimits it externally.

The theatre's maximum diameter is 209 m. The orchestra is 35 m wide. The theatre was able to accommodate some 5400 spectators.

The *cavea* or auditorium, whose concave form is determined by the natural concavity of the hillside, is subdivided radially into nine wedge-shaped sections by eight stairways. Five corridors divide the seating horizontally into orders. Some of the original steps that formed the seating in the central sections have been restored. The wall that delimited the exterior of the *cavea* was pierced by eight doors, each corresponding to one of the stairways that separate the nine sectors of the auditorium.

Externally the *cavea* was delimited by a double portico. The vault of the inner portico supported a tribune or terrace for women spectators. The vault of the outer portico supported a second order of terraces at a higher level; these were intended for the plebs.

The stage of the theatre consisted of a scenic wall enclosing a rear corridor. The wall was pierced by three doors flanked by niches, designed to hold statues. In front of the wall nine columns supported a portico. A second order of 16 columns, in the Corinthian style like the aforementioned ones, adorned the stage. The columns now visible were re-erected, but not in their original positions, during a 19th century restoration. The scenic wall is delimited to the sides by two large rooms (the so-called *parascaenia);* these were designed as a store for the necessary stage equipment and for the use of the actors. This is the residual part of the stage, of which only the wall remains sufficiently well preserved: the *pulpitum* or stage itself was eliminated by the Romans when the theatre was transformed into an amphitheatre.

View of the Greek Theatre.

THE BEACHES OF TAORMINA

The history of Taormina is strictly connected to the nature of the place. The monuments, which illustrate its development, are in perfect harmony with the surrounding landscape. Steep mountains and inaccessible coasts, covered with luxuriant vegetation, wonderful views over the Straits of Messina and beyond it, up to Aspromonte, fantastic promontories and inlets following one after another, all create a backdrop of incomparable beauty.

Along the coast are the beautiful beaches of Mazzarò and Spisone, provided with modern bathing equipment. Before them there is Isola Bella. Between the beach of Mazzarò and that of Isola Bella there is Cape S. Andrea, with fantastic sea grottoes. It can be reached by steps cut into the rock.

Messina

It is the first Sicilian town the tourist meets, if he comes from the continent. Messina is situated between the sea and the first slopes of the Peloritani Mountains, on the Strait which bears its name. It is charming and suggestive thanks to the variety of its landscapes and colours. The history of this town has been interesting and dramatic. The ancient Siculian town called Zancle (sickle) because of the shape of the land strip closing the harbour, became a Greek colony and was called Messana. It became very important during the Byzantine and Norman periods, till it became in the Middle Ages a remarkable humanistic centre thanks to the renowned Basilica of the Holy Saviour of the Greeks. In 1674 the town tried to rebel against the Spanish government, which repressed the rising by killing many people. In the 18th century plagues and earthquakes depopulated the town, which could not flourish again completely during the following century because of the Bourbon tyranny and the cholera which spread in 1854.

The earthquake which, together with a seaquake, took place on December 18, 1908 destroyed almost the whole town.

It was rebuilt in the same area according to a town plan devised by following very strict antiseismic rules. The geometrically squared streets are 12-30 metres broad. All the houses, except the public buildings, are less than 12 metres high.

Today Messina has been further rebuilt after the damage it suffered from the bombardments during the last world war and occupies an area much larger than the ancient town. It is modern and functional and an important trading and tourist centre.

The philosophers Dicearcos (4th century B.C.) and Aristocle (2nd century B.C.), the rhymers Guido and Oddo delle Colonne (13th century), the painter Antonello di Giovanni d'Antonio, better known as Antonello of Messina (15th century) and the historian and politician Giuseppe La Farina (1815-1863) were all born in Messina.

The Cathedral is the greatest monument in the town, built by Roger II during the first decades of the 12th century. It has been rebuilt many times, since it was often damaged by fire, earthquakes and bombardments. The façade still keeps, in its lower part, the original horizontal stripes and the three portals dating back to the late Gothic age. Particularly beautiful is the main one, with its high spire, on whose sides there are lions supporting twisted columns, on which small statues of Angels and Saints rest. The gable in which one can admire the Coronation of the Virgin, was made by the sculptor Pietro da Bonate in 1468. The lunette with the Madonna on a Throne was made by Gian Battista Mazzola and dates back to 1534. The interior of the Cathedral has a nave and two aisles, with a large transept and three apses. Before the Cathedral there is the fountain of Orion, made by Brother Giovanni Angelo Montorsoli, who worked at it from 1547 to 1550. The fountain, with three steps, consists of a polygonal basin, with reliefs representing fantastic animals, on whose brim there are statues representing the Tiber, the Nile, the Ebro and the Camaro, and a pillar sculpted with tritons and naiads, supporting two smaller basins, and on the top the statue of Orion, the mythical founder of the town. The bell-tower, separated from the facade of the Cathedral, rises on the left side. It is 60 metres high and has the biggest mechanical clock in the world.

The Duomo (cathedral).
Detail of the façade and of the Orione Fountain.
The interior of the Duomo.

The Church of the Sacred Annunziata. Below: *The Church of St. Francis and the Temlpe of Christ the King.*

THE REGIONAL ARCHAEOLOGICAL MUSEUM

It was founded at the beginning of the present century and keeps all the artistic finds from the Civic Peloritan Museum and what could be salvaged from the 1908 earthquake.

The garden surrounding the building is rich in sculptures and architectonic remains, including the Neptune from the fountain made by Montorsoli, situated in Piazza d'Unità d'Italia.

The Museum has two storeys with 16 halls, plus a Vestibule and a Courtyard.

The many works of art kept there are very precious.

The halls concern respectively: I - the primitives; II - Antonello of Messina and the Flemings; III - the 16th century artists of Messina; IV/VI - 16th and 17th century works; V - Il Caravaggio; VII - ancient sculpture; VIII - terracottas; IX - sarcophagi; X - marble capitals; Xl - various works; XII - material from destroyed churches and monuments; XIII -various arts, among which Sicilian jewellery; XIV - prints; XV - altar - pieces and furniture; XVI - coins and ceramics.

The Museum keeps precious works of art: the «Polyptych of St. Gregory» by Antonello of Messina; «St. Lucy», attributed to the same author; the «Madonna of Itria», by Bronzino; the «Adoration of the Shepherds» and the «Resurrection of Lazarus» by Caravaggio; «Torso of Ephebe», attributed to Scopas; a bronze lectern, pelican-shaped, of Flemish art; the «Madonna and Child» by Laurana; «Scilla» by Montorsoli, from the fountain of Neptune, where it has been replaced by a copy.

Above: *A mosaic fragment: "Head of the Apostle".*
Below: *Laurana's "Madonna and Child".*

Antonello da Messina's inlaid Poliptych of San Gregorio.

Slab a Tarsia.

Tyndaris

It is a very beautiful tourist rising on the homonymous promontory. It was founded by Denis II in 396 B.C. and called Tyndaris. It was one of the last Greek colonies in Sicily. The archaelogical excavations of ancient Tyndaris show us a town with straight and parallel streets, along which houses and shops rose, and efficient sewers situated under the streets. A Greek Theatre, a Basilica and the Thermae have been brought to light.

Of the Basilica, which was probably only a meeting hall with three storeys and 15 metres high, only the lower storey remains. Outside staircases led to the upper floors.

The Thermae, dating back to the 3rd century B.C., have, soon after the entrance, dressing rooms with floors adorned with wonderful mosaics; then the frigidarium with a basin and the calidarium with a heating system. Not far from the Thermae one can admire the remains of a rich Roman house dating back to the first century B.C. The building opens around the four sides of the peristyle. Each side has 8 columns. The drawing-room or tablinum has painted walls and a floor made of marble tesserae.

The ancient town is surrounded by walls built in various periods, from the 2nd to the 5th centuries B.C. There are also five towers, all very well kept. The two higher towers defended the main gate of the town.

Today there is in Tindari a Museum which keeps archaeological finds and works of art dating back to the Greek and Roman periods. From a Belvedere, situated at 270 metres in height, one can enjoy the view of the wonderful surrounding landscape.

The Sanctuary of the Black Madonna.

Tyndaris: Ruins of the Basilica and of the Roman house.

The Aeolian Islands

They constitute a true Eden, thanks to their peculiar nature, intact landscapes and steep cliffs on an uncontaminated sea. The archipelago is formed by some larger islands, such as Vulcano, Lipari, Salina, situated near one another; and by some smaller ones, such as Panarea, Alicudi and Filicudi.

From their hills one can admire not only the whole archipelago, but also the coasts of Calabria and Sicily and the top of Etna.

Various seismic and volcanic phenomena, more frequent and intense from west to east, take place in all the Aeolian islands. The volcanoes of this area come from the bottom of the sea and successive raisings have brought them to the surface. Archaeological excavations have shown the importance these islands have had since the neolithic age, when man learned how to work obsidian, a volcanic material thrown up by the many craters of the islands, and make various tools, since it is harder and sharper than flint. Most of the prehistoric material found here is kept in the Aeolian Museum of Lipari.

Thanks to their fine situation, the islands became in various periods a safe shelter for pirates, who from here sailed for their raids on the sea and nearby coasts.

Today the inhabitants dedicate themselves mainly to fishing and pumice quarrying and working.

The volcanic nature of the archipelago, which makes it rocky, bare and poor in water, and its mild and dry climate, help the production of a very good wine (Malvasia), which is exported in its entirety.

The architecture of the houses in this archipelago is very peculiar: white houses with only one storey, colourful ceramic floors, and a terrace before each one, with a reed bower. These islands attract many tourists.

MESSINA
CATANIA
SIRACUSA
RAGUSA
ENNA
CALTANISSETTA
PALERMO
TRAPANI
AGRIGENTO

Torre di Faro
Sparti
Rosso
Spadafora
C. di Milazzo
Milazzo
Barcellona
Pozzo di Gotto
S. Lucia del Mela
Castroreale
S. Lucia del Mela
Villafranca T.
S. Teresa di Riva
Giardini
Taormina
Fumefreddo di Sicilia
Riposto
Giarre
Acireale
Aci Trezza
Novara di Sicilia
Francavilla di Sicilia
Randazzo
Linguaglossa
Bronte
Adrano
Paternò
Etna 3263
Nicolosi
Belpasso
Piana di Catania
Lentini
Carlentini
Melilli
Augusta
C. Campolato
C. S. Croce
C. Murro di Porco
Capo Passero
Portopalo
Pachino
Noto
Avola
Ispica
Pozzallo
Rosolini
Modica
Scicli
Marina di Ragusa
Punta Secca
Comiso
Vittoria
Chiaramonte Gulfi
Licodia Eubea
Grammichele
Caltagirone
Mineo
Palagonia
Vizzini
Buccheri
Palazzolo Acreide
Gela
Licata
Niscemi
Mazzarino
Butera
Riesi
Sommatino
Canicattì
Campobello di Licata
Naro
Palma di Montechiaro
Favara
Aragona
Raffadali
Cattolica Eraclea
Ribera
Sciacca
Menfi
Selinunte
Castelvetrano
Mazara d. Vallo
Marsala
Trapani
Erice
Paceco
Favignana
Le Egadi
S. Vito lo Capo
Castellammare d. Golfo
Segesta
Alcamo
Partinico
Monreale
Cefalù
Termini Imerese
Bagheria
Solunto
Corleone
Prizzi
Bivona
Cammarata
Petralia
Castelbuono
Gangi
Nicosia
Troina
Leonforte
Agira
Regalbuto
Centuripe
Piazza Armerina
Villa del Casale
Barrafranca
Pietraperzia

Isole Eolie o Lipari
I. Stromboli
I. Panarea
S. Pietro
I. Salina
Lingua
I. Filicudi
I. Alicudi
I. Lipari
I. Vulcano
Porto Levante

I. Ustica
Pantelleria
I. Pantelleria
Montagna Grande